W9-BMW-588

UNCOMMON COURTESY FOR KIDS

TEACHING THE BASIC RULES OF ETIQUETTE

BY GREGG & JOSH HARRIS

To Joel,
Who is becoming such a fine young gentleman.

Copyright * 1990 by Gregg and Josh Harris

All rights reserved. This book may be photocopied by the original purchaser for personal and household use only. Such reproductions may not be resold. Except for the limited authorization to photocopy. stated above. no part of this book may be reproduced or transmitted in any form or by any means. electronic or mechanical. including photocopying. recording or by any information storage and retrieval system. without permission in writing from the publisher.

Noble Publishing Associates
Vancouver,WA 98685
www.noblepublishing.com
1-800-225-5259

Printed In China
ISBN 0-923463-72-0

TABLE OF CONTENTS

Special pull out Master List folded inside Back Cover

PREFACE

Courtesy has fallen on hard times. No longer can we refer to "common courtesy" because courtesy is no longer common. It is nearly extinct. Why? Because for the last two generations courtesy has not been handed down to children. Our parents assumed that our instructors in school would teach us our manners. They were wrong.

What little effort was made was quickly spurned by most of us because so much of courtesy is based on honoring the differences between people. The elderly, authority figures, women, children, the handicapped and others must be respected in different ways. Living as we did through the civil rights movement, the feminist movement and our own peer groups in the fifties and sixties, our generation got the mistaken impression that it was wrong to acknowledge that such differences exist. Etiquette was accused of being shallow, sexist, pro-establishment and demeaning to the weak. Under those terms, what member of the baby-boom generation would want to have "proper manners"? Better, we supposed, to pool our inexperience and develop our own codes of conduct. The result is what we see today, a confused and uncertain generation, trying to decide which manners, if any, to teach their own children.

Uncommon Courtesy for kids is designed to cut through this confusion and establish a beachhead for basic etiquette in the next generation. If it succeeds your children will shine as lights in the darkness of their ill-mannered age-mates. In this kit I have chosen to restore some old fashioned attitudes, with certain qualifications. I take the position that honoring your elders is not the same thing as believing they are always right. Offering your seat to a woman in a waiting room is not the same as treating her as though she is helpless, and expecting children to be considerate of adults is not the same as asking them to "be seen but not heard." Courtesy in this kit is consideration for the needs and feelings of others. It serves others from a position of personal moral conviction. It does not, like Miss Manners, attempt to establish proper ways of doing morally improper things.

Morris Chalfant has written, "We must choose to be courteous and develop the discipline of courtesy each day. We do not stumble into being a gentleman or lady. The home that has no time for for courtesy will always have time for rudeness. The home that does not take time for compliments will always have time for complaints. The home that has no time for smiles will always have time for frowns. And the home that has no time for sweet loving words will always find time for harsh, critical words."

In other words, there can be no middle ground in this battle. We are either courteous or discourteous, considerate or inconsiderate. Unfortunately, while we, as a generation, come to grips with our own lack of understanding of basic etiquette, our children are growing up with even less of a definition! In many ways our children are like immigrants in their own homes. Like someone who who has just arrived in a new country each child is confused about what he may and may not do in his new surroundings. Unwritten rules seem to define what is acceptable and unacceptable behavior. Trial and error is required to discover the boundaries. And the moods of local authorities seem to change the rules from day to day. A person in this situation needs a trusted friend to teach him the way things work so that he can stay out of trouble and get on with the adventure of life.

Just like the newly arrived immigrant, each child needs an orientation to the rules of basic etiquette— not the kind of sissy stuff that fusses over which fork to use first at a formal dinner. Children, like all the rest of us, need the survival skills level of etiquette to guide them in the major contexts of life on this planet. In the home, in the car, at church, in public places, and so on; these are the settings where children learn to show consideration toward others. And the process of learning courtesy is cumulative. Little by little, as a child hears and sees these rules applied in his daily routine, he becomes sensitized to proper and improper etiquette. He develops a feel for courtesy that serves him for the rest of his life. So as you use this kit, be patient with your child and with yourself. Be consistent, but above all, be courteous.

Many parents already use **The Original 21 Rules of This House** as the basis of social order in their homes and **Rules for Young Friends** as the ground rules for having positive friendships in the neighborhood, church and school. Both kits have been developed by our family and are published by Noble Publishing Associates. If you don't already have them, I suggest that you take advantage of these resources. They are no doubt available from the same outlet where you purchased **Uncommon Courtesy**.

~Thank you for allowing our family to serve your family. May God richly bless you as you train up your children in the way that they should go.

Gregg Harris

Gregg Harris
Gresham, Oregon

PROVERBIAL COURTESY

Proverbs 13:20
He who walks with the wise grows wise, but a companion of fools suffers harm.

Proverbs 12:22
The Lord detests lying lips, but he delights in men who are truthful.

Proverbs 17:14
Starting a quarrel is like breaching a dam; so drop the matter before a dispute breaks out.

Proverbs 26: 18-19
Like a madman shooting firebrands or deadly arrows is a man who deceives his neighbor and says, "I was only joking!"

Proverbs 15:1
A gentle answer turns away wrath, but a harsh word stirs up anger.

Proverbs 18:13
He who answers before listening— that is his folly and shame.

Proverbs 11:27
He who seeks good finds goodwill, but evil comes to him who searches for it.

Proverbs 19:4
Wealth brings many friends, but a poor man's friend— deserts him.

Proverbs 19:17
He who is kind to the poor lends to the Lord, and He will reward him for what he has done.

Proverbs 25:28
Like a city whose walls are broken down is a man who lacks self-control.

Proverbs 13:1
A wise son heeds his father's instruction, but a mocker does not listen to rebuke.

A NOTE FROM THE ARTIST

Dear Parents,

Here we are again! This is my third opportunity to illustrate a coloring book for kids. With my first book, **The Original 21 Rules of This House**, I was a little nervous, but it has received great reviews from parents and pastors. Then, with **Rules for Young Friends** I saw how much parents appreciate good tools to help their children get along well with young guests. Now with **Uncommon Courtesy for Kids** my dad and I are aiming for the biggest challenge of all: proper etiquette!

Our family has been using the **Uncommon Courtesy** rules for quite some time. They have had good effects on all of us. Because they work so well for us, we suspect they will help almost any family.

Learning how to be courteous is great. Everyone enjoys being around people who are kind and considerate. Too bad courtesy has become so uncommon. I hope our rules will help it become much more common in your family.

In Christ,

Joshua

Joshua Harris
(at age 15)

Are There Any Immigrants In Your Home?

In many ways children are like immigrants in their own homes. Like someone who has just arrived in a new country—

- They are confused about what they may and may not do in their new surroundings.

- Unwritten rules seem to define what is acceptable and unacceptable behavior.

- Trial and error is required of them, and the moods of local authorities change the rules from day to day.

Children, like imigrants, must do all this while trying to learn a new language!

The Training and Instruction of the Lord

Ephesians 6:4

Fathers, do not exasperate your children;
instead, bring them up in the training
and instruction of the Lord.

Don't be harsh.

- Don't offend your child's sense of justice by your own
  bad example; instead train and instruct your children
  the same way God trains and instructs His children.

But how does God deal with His children?

Uncommon Courtesy is considering the needs and feelings of others.

Matthew 7:12

*So in everything, do unto others
as you would have them do unto you,
for this sums up the law and the Prophets.*

Philippians 2:3

*Do nothing out of selfish ambition or vain conceit,
but in humility consider others
better than yourselves.*

Uncommon Courtesy is considering the needs and feelings of others.

Make Time for Courtesy

"We must choose to be courteous and develop the discipline of courtesy each day. We do not stumble into being a gentleman or lady. The home that has no time for courtesy will always have time for rudeness. The home that does not take time for compliments will always have time for complaints. The home that has no time for smiles will always have time for frowns. And the home that has no time for sweet loving words will always find time for harsh, critical words."

~Morris Chalfant

The home that has no time for courtesy...

... will always have time for rudeness.

Six Manners of Speech

1. Think clearly about what you are going to say before you speak.

2. Look at others when you are talking to them.

3. Cheerfully say, "Hello" and "Good-bye" to people as they come and go.

4. Say "Please" when you ask, and "Thank you" when you receive any favor.

5. Answer, "Yes, sir" or "No, sir" when speaking to a man and "Yes, ma'am" or "No, ma'am" when speaking to a woman.

6. Speak as clearly and concisely as you can.

Four Words to the Wise

1. **"Pardon me."**
   -Say "Pardon me" when you cause an interruption.

2. **"I'm sorry."**
   -Considerately say, "I'm sorry" when you may have hurt someone.

3. **"I was wrong."**
   -Contritely admit your mistakes. Rather than making excuses, simply say, "I was wrong."

4. **"I forgive you."**
   -Graciously forgive the offenses of others.

Five Rules for Public Transportation

1.   Stay together. Don't run ahead or lag behind.

2.   Hold hands when walking through crowds.

3.   Offer to carry any luggage that you can carry.

4.   Never point at people or comment about their differences.

5.   Don't talk too loudly, laugh too loudly, or stare at others.

Six Ways to be Considerate to Adults

1. Always knock on closed doors and wait for a response before opening them.

2. Rise whenever an adult approaches or enters the room for the first time.

3. Offer your seat to an adult if no other seat is available.

4. Insist on giving your seat to women or elderly people when in a crowded place.

5. Always allow adults (and girls, if you are a boy) to pass through doorways before you.

6. When adults are talking, listen carefully to what they are saying and be prepared to ask a question or give an appropriate response about the same topic.

Six Table Manners

1. Always be clean and neat when you come to the dinner table.

2. Sit at the dinner table without slouching, leaning on the table with your elbows, or tilting your chair back on two legs.

3. Always wait until your mother or the hostess starts eating before you begin.

4. Take only your fair share of any food item and then be sure to eat all that you take.

5. Eat neatly and silently, chewing carefully with your mouth closed; never talk when your mouth has food in it.

6. You may ask to be excused from the table in your own home, but not when you are visiting others.

Phone Manners

1. When answering the phone say, "Hello," in a cheerful voice. Then announce what number the caller has reached.

2. In response to the question, "May I speak to _____?" ask, "Who may I say is calling?"

3. When the caller gives his (or her) name, say, "just a moment, Mr. (or Mrs.) _____; I'll see if my (father/mother) can take your call."

4. After making certain that the person who is receiving the call can take it, return to the phone and say "My (father/mother, etc) will be with you in a moment."

How to Take a Phone Message

1. If the person being called cannot come to the phone, ask the caller if you can take a message and have your father or mother call him/her back.

2. On a phone log or notebook write down the caller's name, phone number, and a few key words to remind you what the call is about.

3. Repeat the entire message back to the caller as you write. Take time to get it right.

4. Say, "Thank you for calling. I will see to it that my (father/mother) gets the message."

5. Deliver the message personally as soon as possible. Don't forget and don't procrastinate.

Seven Rules for Going to Church

1. Prepare for church. Plan ahead to be on time.

2. Focus your thoughts and actions on getting to know God better. You are coming to meet with Him and His people.

3. Be courteous and friendly toward everyone.

4. Do not run, shout, or play roughly inside the building.

5. Pay close attention to what the congregation is doing at any given moment. Follow along as you sing, pray, give, read and listen together.

6. Do not distract others from doing what they should be doing.

7. Show appropriate respect for the church staff, buildings, materials, equipment and grounds.

Eight Rules For Traveling in the Car

1. Wear a seat belt snugly across your lap.

2. Be considerate of other passengers.

3. Speak quietly so as to be heard only by the person or persons to whom you are talking.

4. Do not wrestle or climb over seats.

5. When you are bored, you may suggest a travel game or song for everyone to to enjoy.

6. Patiently wait for rest stops and meals.

7. Clean up your area of the car at the end of every trip.

8. Never stick any part of your body out of the car window.

Four Awkward Things That
Happen to Everybody

1. When you feel a sneeze coming on, cover your nose with your hand or a facial tissue, and make as little noise as possible.

2. When you must cough or yawn, cover your mouth with your hand and say, "Excuse me."

3. When you cannot swallow something at the dinner table, expel it discreetly into your spoon or napkin without comment.

4. When you think you need to groom yourself, never do so in public. To comb your hair, clean your fingernails, or straighten your clothing, go to the lavatory.

Sometimes, Being "Rude" Is the Rule

*There are bad people in the world who
may try to hurt you. Never get into a car
or go anywhere with an adult whom you don't know.*

- Even if he calls you by name.

- Even if he says, "Your mother/father sent me,"

- Even if he says, "Please, help me. I'm lost,"

- Even if he offers you presents of money,
  candy or ice cream.

- Don't talk to strangers. Go home.

Apply Each Rule in a Training Ground

- Your child will learn the rules, little by little, over a period of time. Never rush or become impatient with his progress.

- Post each group of rules, one at a time, on your refrigerator door and read the rules slowly, pointing to each as you say it out loud.

- Make "small things" the training grounds for proper courtesy at all times, even at play.

- Throughout the day, recite the rule to one another. Keep reviewing.

- Reinforce his memory and begin to develop his understanding of each rule by applying it.

- Ward off wrong behavior whenever it starts without nagging or belittling your child.

Example: When you see a child begin to walk away after receiving a favor, smile and quote, "Say, 'Please' when you ask and 'Thank you' when you receive any favor." Be pleasant.

Uncommon Courtesy

Let's face up to the fact that "common courtesy" isn't as common as it used to be! Proper etiquette is practically extinct. Uncommon Courtesy for Kids teaches children 56 ways to be considerate of others. It will help your children understand what to do and what not to do in eleven different situations. This kit covers everything from meal times to going to church. Includes a laminated list of all 56 rules, a reproducible coloring book, and individual posters for each rule.
For ages 3 and up.
Item #1799.........$14⁹⁵

Rules For Young Friends

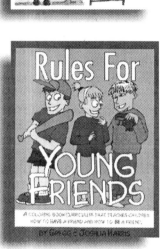

Do you feel overrun by your child's playmates? This valuable resource provides 11 simple rules for friendships. Rules For Young Friends is a coloring book curriculum that will help you teach your child to be a good host and a good guest. In addition to family house rules, this set includes rules for loyalty towards family members, borrowing and loaning toys, friends who interrupt chores and much more. This training kit has worked for thousands of families, and it can work for you.
Item #1042.........$14⁹⁵

The Choreganizer

Overwhelmed by household chores at your house? **The Choreganizer** to the rescue! This valuable tool helps you: **1) Identify all the household chores that need to be done** (with 60 colorful chore cards). **2) Assign them to your children** (on individualized chore charts) and **3) Monitor completion on a daily basis.** Visually appealing and fun to use, it also offers its unique **Chore Store, Mom Money** and **Dad Dollars** giving your children tangible goals to work toward and a way for you to say "thanks for helping."
Item #1725.........$16⁹⁵

WILL YOUR CHILD BE A FOLLOWER OR A LEADER?

Dr. Jeff Myers has found that people who communicate well are chosen to be leaders. His new book *From Playpen to Podium* shows you how to improve your child's communication skills through reading, writing and thinking skills. It also enhances their comfort in social situations, helps them resist negative peer influences, and develops leadership skills. Now you can easily give your children the communication advantage.

Item #1036.........$14⁹⁵

Make Time for Courtesy

"We must choose to be courteous and develop the discipline of courtesy each day. We do not stumble into being a gentleman or lady. The home that has no time for courtesy will always have time for rudeness. The home that does not take time for compliments will always have time for complaints. The home that has no time for smiles will always have time for frowns. And the home that has no time for sweet loving words will always find time for harsh, critical words."

~Morris Chalfant

❶

Six Manners of Speech

1. Think clearly about what you are going to say before you speak.

2. Look at others when you are talking to them.

3. Cheerfully say, "Hello" and "Good-bye" to people as they come and go.

4. Say "Please" when you ask, and "Thank you" when you receive any favor.

5. Answer, "Yes, sir" or "No, sir" when speaking to a man and "Yes, ma'am or "No, ma'am" when speaking to a woman.

6. Speak as clearly and concisely as you can.

②

Four Words to the Wise

1. "Pardon me."
   -Say "Pardon me" when you cause an interruption.

2. "I'm sorry."
   -Considerately say, "I'm sorry" when you may have hurt someone.

3. "I was wrong."
   -Contritely admit your mistakes. Rather than making excuses, simply say, "I was wrong."

4. "I forgive you."
   -Graciously forgive the offenses of others.

Five Rules for Public Transportation

1. Stay together. Don't run ahead or lag behind.

2. Hold hands when walking through crowds.

3. Offer to carry any luggage that you can carry.

4. Never point at people or comment about their differences.

5. Don't talk too loudly, laugh too loudly, or stare at others.

❹

Six Ways to be Considerate to Adults

1. Always knock on closed doors and wait for a response before opening them.

2. Rise whenever an adult approaches or enters the room for the first time.

3. Offer your seat to an adult if no other seat is available.

4. Insist on giving your seat to women or elderly people when in a crowded place.

5. Always allow adults (and girls, if you are a boy) to pass through door ways before you.

6. When adults are talking, listen carefully to what they are saying and be prepared to ask a question or give an appropriate response about the same topic.

5

Six Table Manners

1. Always be clean and neat when you come to the dinner table.

2. Sit at the dinner table without slouching, leaning on the table with your elbows, or tilting your chair back on two legs.

3. Always wait until your mother or the hostess starts eating before you begin.

4. Take only your fair share of any food item and then be sure to eat all that you take.

5. Eat neatly and silently, chewing carefully with your mouth closed; never talk when your mouth has food in it.

6. You may ask to be excused from the table in your own home, but not when you are visiting others.

Phone Manners

1. When answering the phone say, "Hello," in a cheerful voice. Then announce what number the caller has reached.

2. In response to the question, "May I speak to _____?" ask, "Who may I say is calling?"

3. When the caller gives his (or her) name, say, "Just a moment, Mr. (or Mrs.) _____. I'll see if my (father/mother) can take your call."

4. After making certain that the person who is receiving the call can take it, return to the phone and say My (father/mother, etc.) will be with you in a moment.

How to Take a Phone Message

1. If the person being called cannot come to the phone, ask the caller if you can take a message and have your father or mother call him/her back.

2. On a phone log or notebook write down the caller's name, phone number, and a few key words to remind you what the call is about.

3. Repeat the entire message back to the caller as you write. Take time to get it right.

4. Say, "Thank you for calling. I will see to it that my (father/mother) gets the message."

5. Deliver the message personally as soon as possible. Don't forget and don't procrastinate.

8

Seven Rules for Going to Church

1. Prepare for church. Plan ahead to be on time.

2. Focus your thoughts and actions on getting to know God better. You are coming to meet with Him and His people.

3. Be courteous and friendly toward everyone.

4. Do not run, shout, or play roughly inside the building.

5. Pay close attention to what the congregation is doing at any given moment. Follow along as you sing, pray, give, read and listen together.

6. Do not distract others from doing what they should be doing.

7. Show appropriate respect for the church staff, buildings, materials, equipment and grounds.

Eight Rules For Traveling in the Car

1. Wear a seat belt snugly across your lap.

2. Be considerate of other passengers.

3. Speak quietly so as to be heard only by the person or persons to whom you are talking.

4. Do not wrestle or climb over seats.

5. When you are bored, you may suggest a travel game or song for everyone to to enjoy.

6. Patiently wait for rest stops and meals.

7. Clean up your area of the car at the end of every trip.

8. Never stick any part of your body out of the car window.

10

Four Awkward Things That Happen to Everybody

1. When you feel a sneeze coming on, cover your nose with your hand or a facial tissue, and make as little noise as possible.

2. When you must cough or yawn, cover your mouth with your hand and say, "Excuse me."

3. When you cannot swallow something at the dinner table, expel it discreetly into your spoon or napkin without comment.

4. When you think you need to groom yourself, never do so in public. To comb your hair, clean your fingernails, or straighten your clothing, go to the lavatory.

Sometimes, Being "Rude" Is the Rule

There are bad people in the world who may try to hurt you. Never get into a car or go anywhere with an adult whom you don't know.

- Even if he calls you by name.

- Even if he says, "Your mother/father sent me."

- Even if he says, "Please, help me. I'm lost."

- Even if he offers you presents of money, candy or ice cream.

- Don't talk to strangers. Go home.

12